To Rosemary

How Dogs Really Work!

by · Alan · Snow

Collins

An Imprint of HarperCollins*Publishers*

First published in Great Britain by
HarperCollins Publishers Ltd in 1993
First published in this miniature edition in 1994
10 9 8 7 6 5 4 3 2 1
Text and illustrations copyright © 1993 Alan Snow

A CIP catalogue record for this title
is available from the British Library.

The author asserts the moral right to
be identified as the author of the work.

ISBN 0 00 198058-0

Printed and bound in Italy

This book is set in
Snow Pirate Some Serif

Contents

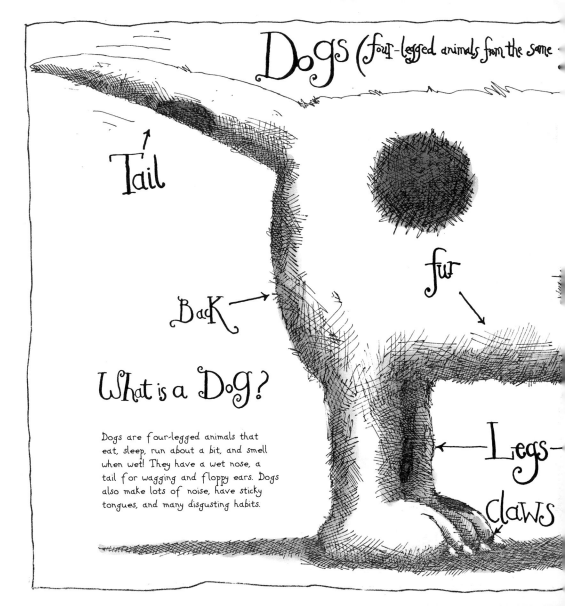

Dogs (four-legged animals from the same

Tail

Back →

fur

Legs

Claws

What is a Dog?

Dogs are four-legged animals that eat, sleep, run about a bit, and smell when wet! They have a wet nose, a tail for wagging and floppy ears. Dogs also make lots of noise, have sticky tongues, and many disgusting habits.

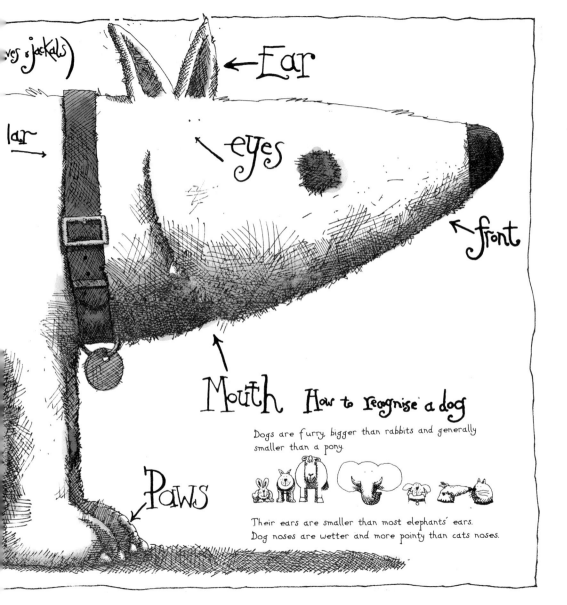

ves & jackals)

← **Ear**

lar →

↖ eyes

↖ front

↑
Mouth

Paws ↙

How to recognise a dog

Dogs are furry, bigger than rabbits and generally smaller than a pony.

Their ears are smaller than most elephants' ears. Dog noses are wetter and more pointy than cats noses.

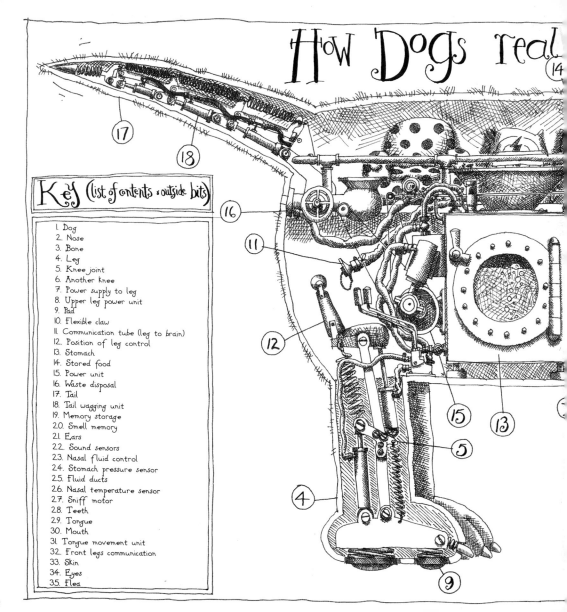

How Dogs real..

Key (list of contents & outside bits)

1. Dog
2. Nose
3. Bone
4. Leg
5. Knee joint
6. Another knee
7. Power supply to leg
8. Upper leg power unit
9. Pad
10. Flexible claw
11. Communication tube (leg to brain)
12. Position of leg control
13. Stomach
14. Stored food
15. Power unit
16. Waste disposal
17. Tail
18. Tail wagging unit
19. Memory storage
20. Smell memory
21. Ears
22. Sound sensors
23. Nasal fluid control
24. Stomach pressure sensor
25. Fluid ducts
26. Nasal temperature sensor
27. Sniff motor
28. Teeth
29. Tongue
30. Mouth
31. Tongue movement unit
32. Front legs communication
33. Skin
34. Eyes
35. Flea

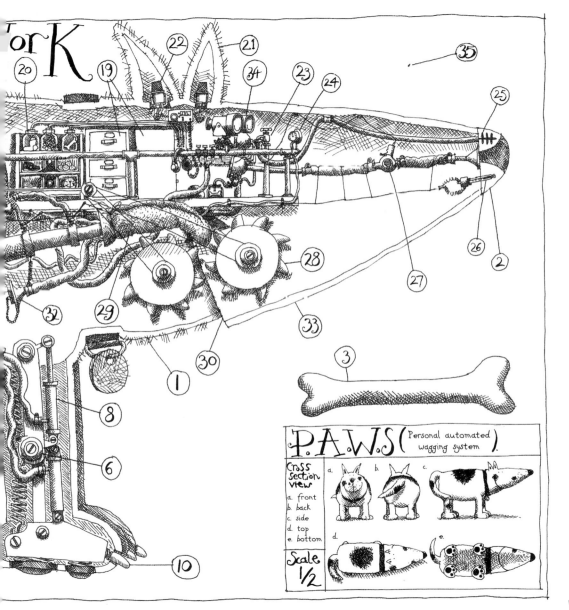

'orK

20
19
22
21
34
23
24
35
25
32
29
30
1
28
27
26
2
33
8
6
3
10

P.A.W.S (Personal automated wagging system)

Cross section views
a. front
b. back
c. side
d. top
e. bottom

Scale 1/2

a. b. c.

d. e.

The Brain an

(Brain, the area in the he

Stored information

←Visual info.

communication link

Stomach pressure monitoring touch

Smell memory

lost information

quick visual reference.

taste information

←Noise Generator

taste→

fluid to tongue

taste sensors

Power to tee

12

ntral Nervous System
(It controls the body!!)

The brain receives information that comes from the senses and uses it to find food, cats and a place to sleep. All the information that goes into the brain is compared with what is already there (memories). The brain then decides what to do and sends messages to the body. This results in a response (see example below).

distributor

← smells

fluid

← smell

temperature sensor

nostril

touch sensors

← teeth

<u>What happens when a dog meets a cat</u>

Dog thinks...
1. "What is this?"
2. "I saw one yesterday."
3. "What shall I do? What did I do yesterday?"
4. "I shall bark at it, because I did that yesterday and it went off so I could sleep in peace."
5. Brain tells body to bark.
6. Cat runs off. 7. Dog goes to sleep.

FOOD, SMELLS & POWER

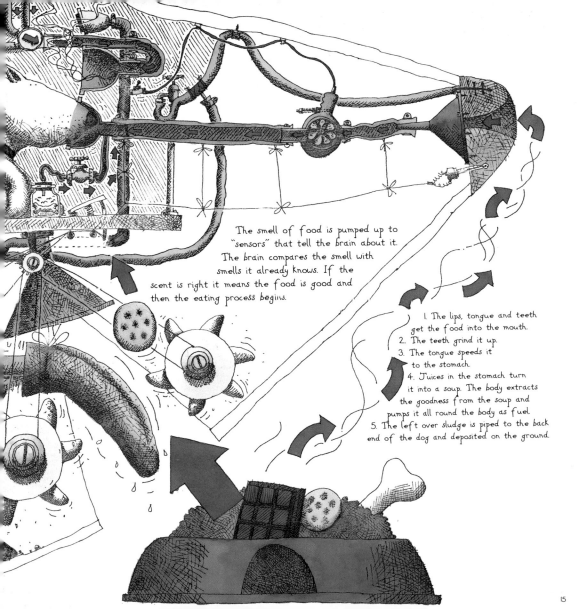

The smell of food is pumped up to "sensors" that tell the brain about it. The brain compares the smell with smells it already knows. If the scent is right it means the food is good and then the eating process begins.

1. The lips, tongue and teeth get the food into the mouth.
2. The teeth grind it up.
3. The tongue speeds it to the stomach.
4. Juices in the stomach turn it into a soup. The body extracts the goodness from the soup and pumps it all round the body as fuel.
5. The left over sludge is piped to the back end of the dog and deposited on the ground.

15

Communication

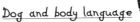

Dog and body language

Making noises, wagging tails or pulling faces are all methods of sending messages. Dogs are no different from other creatures and communicate by the method which seems best at the time.

1. Barking

A loud noise made by pushing air out of the body through the mouth. This is great for scaring cats, postmen and burglars.

2. Wagging

A wobbling of the tail in joy,

3. Eye contact

This scares an opponent off; very useful with cats. Showing teeth at the same time adds a further warning.

What happens when?

The eyes pick up an image of another dog
1. The brain checks it against memories.
Is it a bone? No
Is it a cat? No
Is it a plate of dog food? No
Is it a dog? Yes
Do I know this dog? Yes. His name is Fang and he is my frie
2. All is well and both dogs go about sniffing, barking, burying things and digging other things up.

16

Dogs don't speak English!

You can make dogs understand a few simple words –
such as "food", "walkies" or "cat" – if you speak
clearly and loudly. But dogs will not understand
"No!" or even "If you do that again, I will not
be a happy owner!"

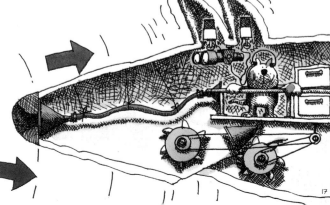

17

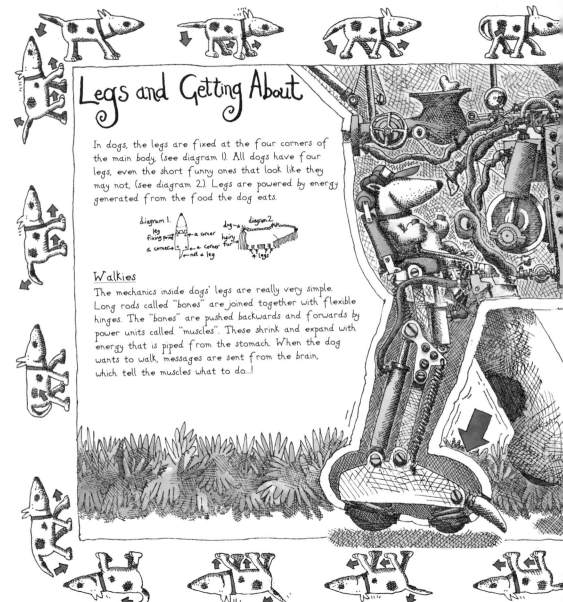

Legs and Getting About

In dogs, the legs are fixed at the four corners of the main body, (see diagram 1). All dogs have four legs, even the short funny ones that look like they may not, (see diagram 2). Legs are powered by energy generated from the food the dog eats.

diagram 1.
leg
fixing point → a corner
a corner → a corner
not a leg

dog → diagram 2
hairy fur
4 legs

Walkies

The mechanics inside dogs' legs are really very simple. Long rods called "bones" are joined together with flexible hinges. The "bones" are pushed backwards and forwards by power units called "muscles". These shrink and expand with energy that is piped from the stomach. When the dog wants to walk, messages are sent from the brain, which tell the muscles what to do...!

The Family Tree

In the days before people started to keep dogs, dogs used live in big family groups called packs. Slowly some of them became friendly with humans. The humans slowly began to develop the dogs to make them more useful, and the dogs became more and more different...some had big noses, some long legs, and others short ears, but most of them were less and less like their great-great-great-grandparents...

OGS AND OWNERS
there any difference?

is often said that "dogs look like their owners!" In fact owners will
uly start to resemble their dogs; the clues are easy to spot.

1. A boring dog will just do the same things all the time.
Result - A dull and boring owner.

2. A pretty pampered dog will make its owner feel ugly and inferior.
Result - The owner will rush off to the beauty salon.

3. A fat, lazy dog will not want to go for walks.
Result - the owner gets fat!

4. A smelly, scruffy dog will pollute its home.
Result - Keep away from this dog, its owner and their house.

5. An interesting and clever dog will drag its owner
to many interesting and surprising places.
Result - An interesting and clever owner!

Do you know any dog owners? Are they like their pets?
Do you have a dog? Are you like it?

The Vet

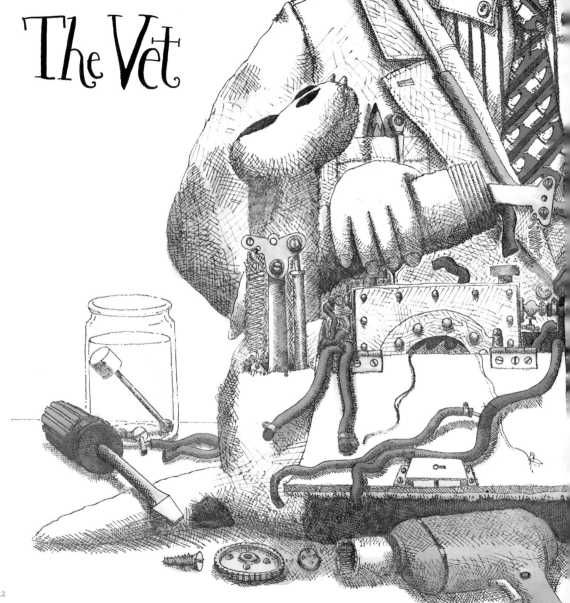

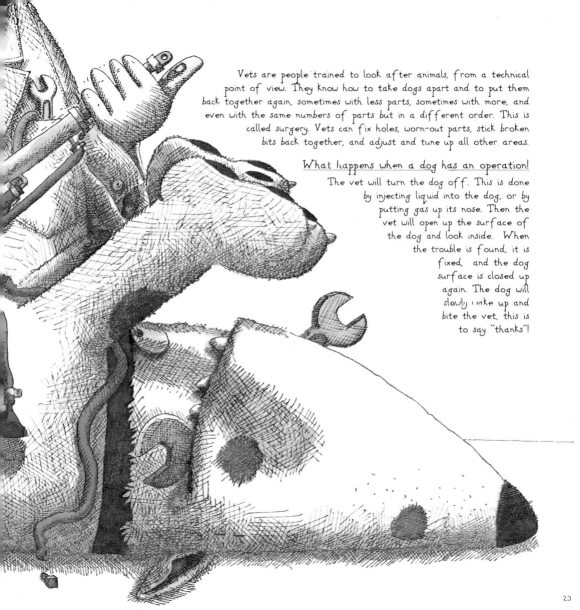

Vets are people trained to look after animals, from a technical point of view. They know how to take dogs apart and to put them back together again, sometimes with less parts, sometimes with more, and even with the same numbers of parts but in a different order. This is called surgery. Vets can fix holes, worn-out parts, stick broken bits back together, and adjust and tune up all other areas.

What happens when a dog has an operation!

The vet will turn the dog off. This is done by injecting liquid into the dog, or by putting gas up its nose. Then the vet will open up the surface of the dog and look inside. When the trouble is found, it is fixed, and the dog surface is closed up again. The dog will slowly wake up and bite the vet, this is to say "thanks"!

General Maintenance

Dogs need fuel! It is what makes them go. Without it they will stop. This is because fuel is turned into power which builds the materials to maintain, and rebuild their structures.

As dogs will eat almost anything put in front of them it is important to control the flow of food into their bodies. If the dog's belly is rubbing on the floor you are probably over-feeding, unless your dog has very short legs. If it starts to try to open cans of food with its teeth, its food intake probably needs checking.

The wrong fuel may affect the dog's performance.

This is not the right fuel.

Keeping your dog undercover at night will make it last longer and keep it in better condition. Failure to do so may badly affect the resale value of your dog.

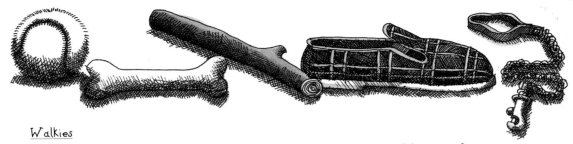

Walkies

It is a good thing to take your dog out for a run once or twice a day as this will keep it in first rate running order. You can test its retrieval mechanisms by throwing a ball or stick and seeing what happens. If the dog goes and gets it, this means all is well. If not, it may mean that:

1. You have thrown it into some nettles.
2. The dog is more interested in almost anything else.
3. It is a boring dog.
4. It is short-sighted.
5. You have forgotten to let go of the stick.

Maintenance chart

PROBLEM	CAUSE	HOW TO FIX
GROWLING	BAD MANNERS OR REDUCED FOOD	THROW FOOD AT IT OR CHANGE DOG'S DIET
FAT + LAZY	OVER FEEDING	EXERCISE OR REDUCE INPUT OF FOOD
THIN + TIRED	OVER EXERCISE	FEED UP

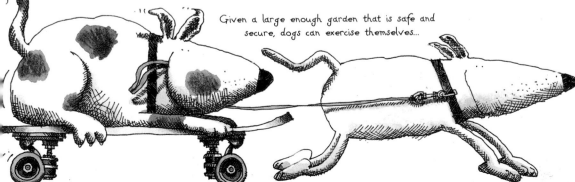

Given a large enough garden that is safe and secure, dogs can exercise themselves...

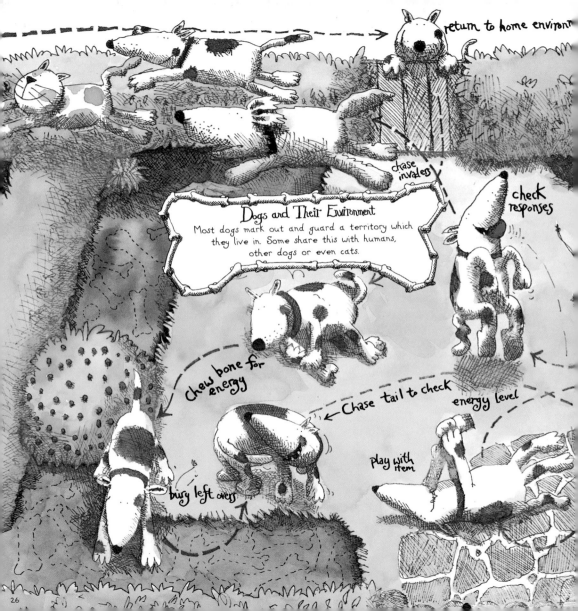

return to home environm

chase invaders

check responses

Dogs and Their Environment
Most dogs mark out and guard a territory which they live in. Some share this with humans, other dogs or even cats.

Chew bone for energy

Chase tail to check energy level

play with item

bury left overs

check for
food sources

revitalize structure

learn skill

explore resources

expel waste

experiment with
environment

Select play item

take in more
energy

The End

Index